WHAT HAVE YOU DONE ALL DAY?

Books by Marjorie Lee

NOVELS

THE LION HOUSE
THE EYE of SUMMER
ON YOU IT LOOKS GOOD
DR. BLOCK and the HUMAN CONDITION

POETRY

WHAT HAVE YOU DONE ALL DAY?

WHAT HAVE YOU DONE ALL DAY?

POEMS BY

MARJORIE LEE

DRAWINGS BY MARILYN MILLER

CROWN PUBLISHERS, INC.   NEW YORK

Most of these poems appeared originally in the *Ladies' Home Journal*; others appeared first in *Good Housekeeping, McCall's, The Saturday Evening Post, The Christian Science Monitor, Redbook, Cosmopolitan,* and elsewhere.

Special acknowledgment is made to Arthur Godfrey, Peter Lind Hayes, and Dinah Shore for their performances of several on radio and television; to Felicia Sanders and Martha Wright for their inclusion of several others on records; and to General Music Publishing Company, Inc., for several poems that appeared as songs.

Library of Congress Catalog Card Number: 73-82946
ISBN: 0-517-506041

ISBN: 0-517-50605X
Printed in the United States of America
Published simultaneously in Canada by General Publishing Company Limited
Designed by Doug Anderson

The poems belong to
Bob and the kids;
and the book belongs
to Jonesie

PREFACE

Now, at the time of the compilation of these verses, Robert is twenty-six, Alison is twenty-five and married, Steve is twenty-three, Jordan is eighteen, and John is fourteen. I, needless to say, am no longer "nearly twenty-six"—as stated in the next-to-the-last line on page 26.

Perhaps this collection should be introduced by one of its verse titles: "Duck! Here Comes That Pendulum Again!" Or maybe this is not so much the return of a lost attitude as it is an awakening of one which, napping temporarily, has been there all along, a possum, merely blanketed by the concepts of our various and sundry American revolutions.

Actually, I'm in favor of ideological revolutions when they lead to new insights, productive freedoms, and fair deals. What gets me down, though, is the slick, intellectualized little bombs that are being dropped on the rooftop of what is now being called The Nuclear Family. Fine, very interesting; yet, for the long, long pull—what have you got that's better?

As for Women's Lib—it's happening. But where it has to happen most is inside.

M. L.
March, 1973

CONTENTS

I What Have You Done All Day?

II Songs for Robert & Co.

III Home, Hearth, and Him

IV For a Child, Leaving

I

WHAT HAVE YOU DONE ALL DAY?

WHAT HAVE *YOU* DONE ALL DAY?

By the time he comes home in the evening,
My Hero, my Man of Affairs,
I have laundered three loads in the washer,
I have made thirty trips on the stairs;
I have vacuumed the rugs and the sofa,
I have waxed the linoleum floors,
I have spent an approximate lifetime
Getting fingerprints wiped from the doors;
I have eight times rediapered my daughter,
And eleven times lifted my son;
I have kicked him his first little football
At the point of his first little gun;
I have battled the beds and the bathtubs,
I have mastered the mop and the broom,

2

I have fixed me a lunch for a princess
Which I somehow forgot to consume;
I have vied with a traveling salesman
And two vendors of new magazines,
I have broken the bank for the butcher,
I have patched me a hole in my jeans;
I have soothed, I have salved, I have bandaged,
I have darned, I have knit, I have purled
By the time he comes home in the evening,
My Hero, my Man of the World;

And it's then that he kisses my forehead
In his tenderest, gentlest way,
And I listen for forty-five minutes
While he tells me he's had a hard day . . .

DON'T ASK ME WOULD I TRADE THEM

FOR A DIAMOND MINE

They're precious in the morning
When they waken me and charm me
With their voices pitched as sweetly
As the whole Apache army,
And they're very cute at lunchtime
In a shooting war of limas
And at supper, playing Discus Thrower
With their Aunt Jemimas—

Oh, they're precious and they're very cute,
    As I've already said;
But I love them best at eight o'clock
    (That's when they go to bed).

I didn't prize that chair they broke,
I didn't like that kettle;
I never used those coasters
That they melted down for metal;
We didn't need that window
Where they knocked the leaded panes in;
It's really quite refreshing
When it snows and sleets and rains in—

    Oh, they're precious and they're very cute
        As I'm the first to say;
    But I love them best at eight o'clock
        (That's when they hit the hay).

What matter if my Gucci shoes
Are used to mix the fudge in?
What matter if a trail of mud
Is tracked each time they trudge in?
Who cares about the bedsheets
That were filched to build a tent up,
Or about the Mason jars in which
Three garter snakes were pent up?

    Oh, they're precious and they're very cute,
        And surely it's no crime
    To love them best at eight o'clock
        (Till then I haven't time).

WINTER: MATERNAL VERSION

Oh, Winter's a wonderful season:
   Consider the breathtaking sight
When the sky is as blue as a bluebird
   And the road is a ribbon of white . . .

(Don't kick when I snap your galoshes;
Stop squirming all over my knees;
Undress: we forgot the four sweaters . . .
Hey, why don't I just let you freeze?)

Oh, Winter's a fabulous season:
   Consider the poets who sing
Of the weather as clear as an ice cube
   And the wind with the whip of a wing . . .

6

(Quit eating the thumb off your mitten;
Your muffler's jammed into your sleeve;
There's a shoelace that's caught in the zipper.
And your foot's in your hat, I believe . . .)

Oh, Winter's a beautiful season:
  Consider the glittering mass
Of the icicles hung from the willow
  And the lawn like a blanket of glass . . .

  And consider its charm for a mother
  Who from morning till night goes about
  The stuffing of kids into snowsuits—
  To say nothing of digging them out.

WARNING TO GREEKS AND OTHER

GIFT-BEARING INDIVIDUALS

O in-laws, friends, and loving ones,
Never give my children guns:
Holstered arms on leather straps,
Silver pistols packed with caps,
Bazookas, BBs, beans, and burps
Crocketts, Boones, and Wyatt Earps,
Tommy, atom, cowboy, cop,
Or pop.

For my first, through my fifth born,
Kindly do not choose a horn;
Nor for their leisure hours alone
Present them with a xylophone;
Resist piano, cymbals, drum
For something they can't strike or strum;
Tempt not my little brood of Jukes
With ukes.

8

Playthings labeled *Just like Real*
Please return or else conceal:
Dolls that cry and wet like babies,
Dogs that bark and carry rabies,
Organ-grinders, carousels,
Ferris wheels equipped with bells,
Bowling alleys, rocket missiles,
Whistles.

Pray lend an ear, O kind and fair—
(My own are shot beyond repair):
If records be the gift unshakable,
Buy *short*-playing, *non*-unbreakable;
Pick perhaps the silent puzzle
Accompanied by gag and muzzle;
Why today, forgot, forsook,
The book?

L'envoi

Grandma, Grandpa, wealthy Unc,
Take it easy on the junk:
And keep in mind when choosing toys—
No noise!

9

JUST LUCKY, I GUESS

We've a backyard with a sandbox,
And a newly fixtured cellar
And a patio and pool deck
Fit for any Rockefeller;
So they've space their drums to beat on
And their little bells to chime in—
But they're bound to choose the area
That I'm in.

When I sit with classic novel
Set for cultural battalions
All its characters start moving
To the lope of Western stallions;
Lined before the television
Are a sofa, stool, and high chair—
But of course it's still essential
To use my chair.

My boys are independent
And my girls are quite resourceful,
Or so hired victims tell me
When I've warned them to be forceful:
Says the sitter, "They were angels,
And we've had a *quiet* time home."
What, I ask, brings forth the massacre
When I'm home?

Raise a cheer for modern mothers
Who can plan their hours of leisure
In a cell of self-seclusion,
Rapt with solitary pleasure—
But with me it could be Shanghai,
Or a coastline Bali Balian,
A castle walled with marble
Of dimensions Taj Mahalian;
A stadium by Lewisohn
For record-breaking quotas,
Or two ranches where the cattle graze
In both of the Dakotas,
Or three mansions flanked by meadows
Borrowed from the King of Siam—
*They would still elect to congregate
Where I am.*

THOUGHTS ON THE CHRISTMAS VACATION

Lover, the logs are aflaming,
    And the holly wreath's hung on the door,
And the mistletoe nods from the ceiling,
    And the tree is set firm on the floor;
Lover, the forests are gleaming,
    And the meadows are white with the Yule;
Lover, the season of Peace is upon us—
    (Lover, the kids have no school).

Sit by me, dearest, and rest you
    From your chores at the wheel and the helm;
And hark to the bells chiming carols
    From the church down at Sedgwick and Elm;
For the turkey is gone, and the puddings
    That your mother once taught me to bake;
Sit by me, dearest; the world lies asleeping
    (Dearest, the kids are awake).

There is joy in the universe, darling,
　　And the angel twinks bright on the bough,
And the gifts of the Magi could hardly surpass
　　What is heaped at our fireplace now;
And the blessings, my darling, the blessings:
　　For three weeks the kids will be home . . .
Darling, I wonder—next Christmas vacation
　　How's for Majorca or Rome?
How's for Siberia,
Iraq, or Syria?
　　How's for New Guinea or Nome?

DON'T WORRY A BIT ABOUT JUNIOR

Don't worry a bit about Junior;
He's normal as normal can be.
    When he purples with rage
    It's a Natural Stage
(It says so on page thirty-three).

Why rant when he samples my perfume?
It proves that he's truly Alert.
    Why pale when he blisters
    The hides of his sisters?
It's merely a Need to Assert.

14

It's fine when he climbs in the closets
And dives from the uppermost shelf;
    It's great when he scrawls
    His designs on the walls,
For he's really Expressing Himself.

Shout huzzahs for the Freudian mater
And her book on the widest of cults,
    Which proclaims in clear phrasing
    The theory amazing
That children are Little Adults;

And don't worry a bit about Junior,
For he's normal as normal can be;
    It's a cinch he'll grow Able,
    Adjusted and Stable—
But what's going to happen to me?

DUCK! HERE COMES THAT PENDULUM AGAIN!

My mother taught me to retreat
From tantrums and domestic treasons
With flat of hand upon my seat;
I give my children Reasons.

For every word I spoke in hate
Said seat acquired a further lesson;
Today my five retaliate
With gems of Self-Expression.

I thought my mother rash and wrong;
But as things go, before much longer
It's certain as a raven's song
My brood will think me wronger.

17

WELCOME FOR A WELCOME THIRD

With the first one they offered me couches:
"Stretch out, you poor dear," they cajoled.
With the second the males slowly rose from their chairs:
"You had better sit down," I was told.
    But my days in the limelight are over;
        Just a fabulous fable of yore;
    And now when I'm out for a night at a party
        I park on the floor.

18

For the first one they ordered a nightie
Made in Paris, all silken and sweet.
For the second they sent us a shirt and a sacque
That they bought in a sale down the street.
    But our days in the limelight are over;
        So, however remiss or remote,
    We'll be gracious and grateful as grateful can be
        If they drop us a note.

Now, the first one was named for his father:
A Junior—traditional, pure.
And the second was Alison: slightly too-too
And a trifle bizarre, to be sure.
    But our days in the limelight are over,
        And our energy's starting to go—
    So don't be surprised if you hear that the third one
        Emerges as Joe.

True, the first's a mechanical wizard:
Surely destined for old M.I.T.
And the second, who shows intellectual genius,
Will probably publish at three.
    But our days in the limelight are over;
        Our ambitions more mellowed and mild—
    And we'll sigh with relief if our precious wee third one
        Is only a child.

II

SONGS FOR ROBERT & CO.

FIRST SONG FOR ROBERT

He's mine, said a sycamore,
    Green and tall;
He's not! sang a whippoorwill—
    Not at all!

He's mine, said a butterfly
    On the vine;
Not so! cried a squirrel—
    I say he's mine!

Ho hum, sighed a rosebud
    Dreamily—
He may be yours . . .
    But he looks like me!

SECOND SONG FOR ROBERT

Ask me why a shadow
   Lies blue upon the snow,
Or who paints the hollyhocks—
   I wouldn't know.

Ask me why the morning
   Turns the moon away,
Or where a dream goes when it ends—
   I couldn't say.

Ask me why a daffodil
   Drinks from a yellow cup—
Mothers don't know everything;
   I'd have to look it up.

All that I can tell you
   Is this, and I will:
When I watch you sleeping
   The world grows still,
And deep down inside me
   I can hear a little ring
Like the laughter of a rabbit
   When the grass calls, "Spring!"

JUST ASK FOR ROBERT

If you're fond of stars
And you've looked about
And you've found the stores
Have run clear out,
There's a high, high hill
Where the roadways cross;
   Just ask for Robert—
He knows the Boss.

If your daydream order
Is overdue
And you'd like some extras
To see you through,
There's an elf in the elm
With a suitcase full;
   Just ask for Robert—
He's got pull.

If you think that Spring
Got tired here
And isn't coming
Back next year . . .
Don't let such trifles
Discontent you;
   Ask for Robert—
Say I sent you.

FOR ROBERT, CONVERSING

I know it isn't Arabic
When Robert tries to speak;
It's not as deep as Russian,
Nor as classical as Greek.
   It's the soft sound, the little sound
   Made by little things:
   The chuckle of a cricket,
   And the flip of sparrow wings;
   It's the sneezes of a honeybee
   With pollen up his nose,
   Or the footsteps of a beetlebug
   Who's walking on his toes . . .
And how am I to study it
By adjective and noun
When with all the books on languages
They've never put it down?
Oh, how am I to understand
This Lilliputian lore—
I, at nearly twenty-six
And five feet four?

FOR ROBERT, GROWING

How big is Robert?
   Two Teddy bears tall;
One medium bounce
   Of a red rubber ball;

The length of a riddle
   Plus one long laugh;
The height of two roses—
   (No, two and a half.)

One pussy willow,
   (A near-grown sprig);
Or seven Popsicles—
   That's how big . . .

Think of the wonders
   Of looking around
Twenty-nine kisses
   Away from the ground!

FOR ROBERT, GOING PLACES

Where is Robert going
  With his steady crawl
Clear across the nursery,
  Out into the hall?

  It could take a year to Rio
  If you went by knee and hand,
  And there's no way to Trinidad
  All by land;
  Oh, it couldn't be Caracas,
  And it couldn't be Kildare,
  And it wouldn't be to Mexico—
  (Too many tourists there.)

But whatever destination,
  And wherever Robert goes,
From his look of plan and purpose
  It's a cinch *he* knows;
And who am I to question
  In such an uppish way
When after all it's doubtful
  If anyone can say
Just where he's going,
Or just where she's going,
Or where *anybody's* going
  On this bright Spring day!

FOR ROBERT, FRIGHTENED

A jagged sound, rending the air,
   Too sharply heard;
A barking dog, a slamming door,
   A word;

The hand of night, casting its forms
   About your bed,
Draping familiar sunlit sills
   With dread;

These are the unexpected springs
   Of childhood fears
That come to fill your wakeful eyes
   With tears.

Call to me then, your tower of strength,
   Your pillar of stone . . .
(There's time to learn that mothers have
   Fears of their own.)

FOR ROBERT, WALKING

Robert's on his feet at last;
    All about the town
He darts and reels with drunken joy.
    (He's up! He's down . . .)

Touched by winds, bewitched he is,
    Ecstatic as a pup;
The world awaits his bouncing step.
    (He's down . . . He's up!)

FOR ROBERT, BATHING

Oh, Robert in his brimming bath's
    A tossing ship upon the seas,
And I am but the galley slave
    Assigned to face and hands and knees.

A tidal wave's a paltry thing
    Compared with waves in Robert's tub,
And two weeks' wash is easier
    Than Robert's elbows are to scrub . . .

Oh, strange it is and odd it is
    That I'll be old before I'm thirty,
Shining up a little boy
    Who's ten times cuter when he's dirty.

RAGOUT ROBERT

A side of sunbeam,
  A slice of moon,
The round of a Springtime
  Afternoon,

Sautéed in honey
  From daffodil jars,
Seasoned to taste
  With a sprinkling of stars,

Braised by a firefly's
  Flickerings,
Garnished with shadows
  Of whippoorwill wings,

C'est délicieux;
  Ah, c'est unique!
C'est utterly, thoroughly
  Magnifique!

Strictly for angels
  With *savoir faire,*
This Ragoût Robert
  (Pronounced *Ro-bair).*

FOR ROBERT & CO.

The hooded coat with satin bows
Is suddenly too tight to close;
The cap that seemed too big for years
Will barely cover Robert's ears;
The canvas stroller in the hall
Is much too narrow, much too small;
And all the rompers, white and blue
And green and yellow, looking new
As on the day they left the store,
Are waiting, waiting in the drawer . . .

Who is the fledgling, now a shade,
A wing-beat in the quiet glade,
Who will in time ride through the town's
Bright streets in Robert's hand-me-downs?

FIRST SONG FOR ALISON

Robert is a sturdy one,
   Strong and growing tall;
Can reach the table when he tries—
   But Alison is small.

Robert's learned his way around;
   He has his language, too;
Can hold his spoon, and walk alone—
   But Alison is new.

Less and less in need of me,
   Free, and doing fine,
Robert is the world's child—
   But Alison is mine!

CHEZ ALISON

The walls are pink with roses,
  A special kind of bloom
That holds the breath of Summertime
  In Alison's room.

And the windows looking outward
  Where squirrels and chipmunks run
Are framed in clouds of organdy
  Chez Alison.

There's an armchair striped like candy,
  And a little white bed
With a rabbit-bordered pillow
  For a small, small head . . .

Oh, it's absolutely certain,
  And it's positively clear;
Why, you'd know it fast as anything:
  A little girl lives here.

SHOPPING LIST FOR ALISON

What do we need for Alison?
  Not a blanket, not a hat,
Not a bunting tied with bows
Nor woolen booties for her toes—
  She's got that.

What do we need for Alison?
  A gentle voice, and quiet ways;
Perhaps a robin round with song—
And she could use a sunlit throng
  Of Summer days.

What do we need for Alison?
  A love from Summer 'way past Fall;
And while you're shopping, just for kicks,
Ask for a dream-boat, three by six—
  That's all.

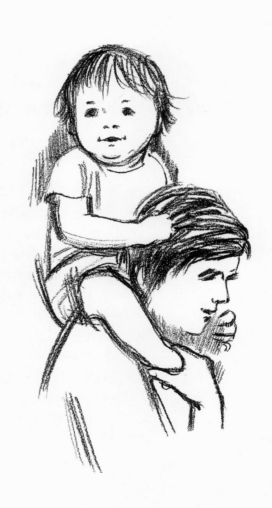

FOR ALISON, WINNING

Another woman's hit this town
Whose eyes upon her father's eyes
Can turn him to a grinning clown
Who once was sensible and wise.

Our household fund, planned tight and square
To cover costs of soup and chops
And light and heat and shoes to wear,
He squanders now on lollipops.

She has an edge of age on me,
And surely he will drive me wild
By reprimanding gallantly,
"Well, after all—she's just a child!"

Of course I lose my battle, then,
To discipline, to sanely judge,
For daughters have a way with men
That Heaven and Hell will never budge . . .

But while I beam and fondly think
Upon this combo strong and stout,
The day she beats me to that mink,
I firmly vow—I'm moving out!

FIRST SONG FOR STEVEN

I never saw the road so wide
As on the day Steve took a ride,
Nor knew a maple half as tall,
As crimson-leafed in any Fall;
And who is there so worn, so cold,
As now could tell me, "Fall is old!"
Or: "Autumn skies are *always* clear!"
Or: "Maples crimson *every* year!"
   There's no such thing as common fare
   When Steven reaches in the air
   To catch a sunbeam; every part
   Of life is new, and at its start . . .
Steel-eyed Cynic, hold your tongue
That all the world is oversung;
How can a place become a bore
Where nothing has been done before?

40

FOR STEVEN, AT THREE

Singing sounds have turned to words;
  Thought sets firmly on the face;
The hop-and-skip, the pitter-pat
  Are now become a steadier pace.

All so swiftly, all so sure
  The change occurs: the clock careens,
And magically the pastel suit
  Is transformed to a pair of jeans.

Who was it leaped the sill last night,
  Popped inside with elfin joy,
Whisked our baby from his bed
  And left instead a little boy?

FOR STEVEN, PLANNING

Today it's fishing in the pond,
    Tonight some other treat;
Tomorrow, if the Fates are fond,
    The tasting of a sweet;

And all the while great men convene,
    Stolid among their chores,
To set the universal scene,
    The politics, the wars . . .

Which plan is first in station
    At God's official throne:
The roarings of a nation,
    Or a small boy's ice cream cone?

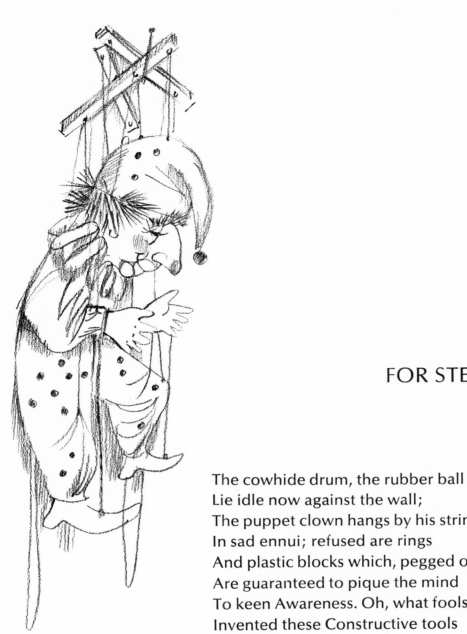

FOR STEVEN, PLAYING

The cowhide drum, the rubber ball
Lie idle now against the wall;
The puppet clown hangs by his strings
In sad ennui; refused are rings
And plastic blocks which, pegged or lined,
Are guaranteed to pique the mind
To keen Awareness. Oh, what fools
Invented these Constructive tools
When Steven neither understands
Nor *wants* Coordinated Hands!
    Day of reckoning, day of woe!
    Where will Advertising go?
    Day of regretting, day to rue!
    What will all the Experts do?
Here is the culprit, here the cad
Who never read a toy-shop ad,
Under the aspen, quite alone,
Playing with leaves and common stone . . .

43

FOR STEVEN, LAUGHING

The headlines stand in solemn black
Like jailors at the nation's back;
The rails are shut, the miners strike—
But Steven's laughing on his bike.

While prices rise and ships go down
An angry river floods a town;
Somewhere a siren screams at dawn—
But Steven's laughing on the lawn.

They're fighting mad on foreign shores,
As coins are flipped to wager wars;
Oh, sorrow lives and love is dead—
But Steven's laughing in his bed.

Just how it is in all this sea
Of tears and fears and enmity
That laughter like a shining bell
Shall stay to spread its breathless spell
Is something neither you nor I
Nor any man can prophesy;
Is something vast, and deep, and odd,
Known by little boys and God.

BOY ON BIKE

(For Steven)

Around the bend an army comes,
Minus bugles and minus drums—
Only the whoosh of the pedaling heels,
And the whirring,
    the wonderful whirring of wheels;
And the flags are missing—but oh, the hues
Of the shirts and the socks and the saddle shoes,
And the studded belts and the cowboy ties,
And the brightness,
    the beautiful brightness of eyes . . .
And I, as I pause from a noontime chore
And stand for a while in the open door,
Watch as the riders go streaking down
In a madcap race to the nearby town;
And watch as I wait for the proud, proud sign
Of a wave of the hand from the one who's mine!

FIRST SONG FOR JORDAN

Little is my littlest love:
    As little as the feet of rain
That creep along the ways of Spring
    To meet against a windowpane;

As little as a buzz of bees,
    And littler still than cooing of
A pigeon waking in the eaves—
    So little is my littlest love,

Who makes of me her little world,
    And of my breast her little hill
Whereon she wanders in the sunlight,
    Gathering flowers where she will.

FOR JORDAN, LEARNING

What shall I tell you
   On the day
The neighbors' children
   Go away,
The kitten grows
   And moves along,
The crickets cease
   Their Summer song?

How shall I make you
   Understand
That snowflakes melt
   Within the hand,
That Heaven's distant—
   Much too far
For any child
   To touch a star?

Oh, what ways
   Can I devise
To let Believing
   Light your eyes?
And should I find them,
   If I could . . .
Would it be wise?
   Would it be good?

FOR JORDAN, DINING

This is the time,
   This is the place
Where Etiquette
   Sits in disgrace;
Where no one ever
   Heard of things
Like knives and forks
   And napkin rings.

Oh, beaten bean,
   Oh, battered beet,
Who says that you
   Were meant to eat?
It's hard to fathom
   Where there's more—
In Jordan's mouth,
   Or on the floor!

FOR JORDAN, ANGRY

Her beating fists, the stamping of her shoes
Resound like tiny drums from wall to wall;
Her fragile throat gives forth the piercing news
Of what she wants (or does not want at all).
Her hair, the shade of caterpillar down,
Flies up in orange clouds about her head,
While fire turns her eyes a blazing brown.
No, no! she shouts her wrath. *No, no, I said!*

What is the sea that washes at my feet
This miniature but oh so perfect rage?
From where this storm, so small, yet so complete,
Unmatched by epic film or classic page,
Which, spent of fury, half a moment after,
Bathes all my world in sudden sunlit laughter?

FIRST SONG FOR JOHN

John has emerged
  from the sea in me,
    from the rounded deeps
      and the gentle swells,
        and his eyes are the blue
        of the sea's own blue,
        and his ears are the scallops
        of nacre shells.
Small as the bud
of an aqueous flower's
the curve of his mouth,
  and the slow uncurl
    of his fists is the blooming
      of aqueous leaves,
        and the stem of his sex
        is a coralline swirl.
        Ashimmer, adripping,
        he slipped from the reef
of my bone and my flesh
and was lifted upon
the shore of the world
  where he drank of the air,
    where he ceased to be Fish,
    and began to be John.

FOR JOHN, CRYING

Rain on rooftops,
   Frost advancing;
Every day
   Is not for dancing.

Bluebells brown
   And done with ringing;
Every day
   Is not for singing.

This I knew,
   But now more clearly:
Joy must not
   Be held too dearly;

Life sets little
   Worlds ashaking;
Small hearts have
   Their share of breaking.

FOR JOHN, CREATING

The world of Art lies at command
Of colors in a grubby hand.
What power in that purple streak;
How modern is this fresh technique.

The freedom of an aesthete's mind
Must not be thwarted or confined,
So stroke away, my busy friend:
Let genius serve its own great end;

Give answer when the Muses call . . .
But keep those crayons off the wall!

FOR JOHN, REALIST

Johnny, Johnny, small and fey,
Was anything but that today;
Was anything but wrapped in schemes
Transported from a world of dreams.
    Whoever knew a single elf
    Who spoke so firmly to himself?
    A wingèd sprite borne by the skies
    With such directness in his eyes?
    What leprechaun in all the land
    Has half the steadiness of hand
    That Johnny has? I must declare
    I've never seen one anywhere,
    Not anywhere, not any place,
    So clear of mind, so sure of face.
And well I wonder, as I should,
About these tales of fairyhood;
Can I expect him to believe
These songs of stardust that I weave?

This magic and this fantasy —
Is it for Johnny . . . *or for me?*

III

HOME, HEARTH, AND HIM

HISTORY, HOME-STYLE

The Bastille fell July fourteenth
In seventeen eighty-nine;
In seventy-six the Colonists
Broke through the British line;
Across the world the Morse Code clicked
In eighteen forty-four . . .
Last April tenth the tulips bloomed
Outside my cellar door.

Elizabeth reigned long and lone
In proud autonomy;
And Antoinette grew beautiful
On pearls and cakes and tea;
In immortality's great tomb
Their royal spirits cool . . .
Today my son brought me a crown
He made at nursery school.

Oh, History, a giant bird,
Wings through the skies of Time;
And wars are won and hearts are lost
While cultures crash or climb;
But I know not of aeons' change,
Nor yet of kingdoms' sway . . .
I live within a lesser house;
I love from day to day.

PORTRAIT OF A CERTAIN MARRIED MAN

He drops his socks upon the floor;
He leaves agape his closet door.
To take his shower, shave his cheek,
He uses twenty towels a week.
　　He rarely wears my Christmas tie;
　　My birthday comes, and passes by;
　　He never brings me bonbon, book,
　　Bouquet; nor mentions how I look.
He irks me like the common cold,
And chills me like a Jello mold;
He piques me like a hornets' swarm;
He glooms me like a thunderstorm.
　　He's arsenic, he's cyanide,
　　The golem monster, Hr. Hyde;
　　He's Jack the Ripper, Mack the Knife,
　　The bane of all my ordered life:
　　The rain the day the picnic's set,
　　And things I haven't thought of yet—
　　Like hiccup, hangnail, scanless sonnet,
　　Fly in oinment, bee in bonnet,
Iron fist in velvet glove—
In toto: *he's the man I love.*

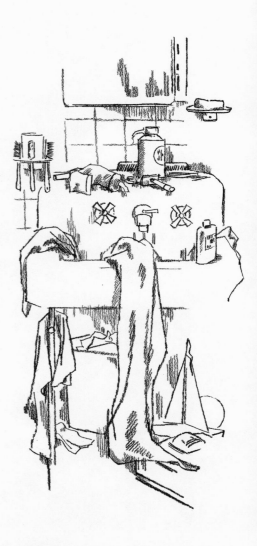

SECOND SPRING

All is as it was before;
Nothing less, and nothing more:
Maples in a happy stir,
Willows as they always were;
Budded limb and flowered stem—
Nothing came to alter them;
Clicking hum the crickets make,
Little songs for Springtime's sake.

April prettily arranged—
Nothing new, and nothing changed,
Save for me and save for you:
We have grown an inch or two.

SUBURBAN SONG

Of all the sounds, enchanting, clear,
That fall upon suburban ear—
A bark of dog, a hum of bee,
A burst of robins, April-free,
A church bell, sonorous and sweet,
Winging its way from Maple Street,
A splash of hoses, fresh as dawn,
A whir of mowers on the lawn,
A tree-saw and a model plane,
The whistle of a distant train,
A cricket clicking out its code,
And children shouting in the road—

Of all the sounds that stop and start
And make a music in my heart,
The best occurs at half past five:
A car that turns into the drive,
Brakes smartly in the evening gloam,
And tells me that my love is home.

THE BIRD IN THE ILEX

There's a nest in the ilex
At the door,
And when school is out
And a child runs through
The door whangs open
And clatters to.

The bird in the ilex
On her eggs
Is shot with fear
When a child bangs by
And flutters her wings
With a startled cry.

"Look into the ilex
From a stool,"
I tell my child,
"And consider the plan
Of life in a world
Of bird and man."

But the nest in the ilex,
Dry as hay,
Has long been left;
And the eggs alone
Are silent tokens
Of bird-blue stone.

For a child at an ilex
Is no friend;
And the swing of a door
Is a sharp rebuff;
And love, for a bird,
Is not enough.

HOMEMADE VALENTINE

All of my life seems a little thing,
    Plus a little thing, plus a little more:
A sock to darn, and a rake to buy
    At the hardware store;

A Sunday brunch, and a Sunday ride,
    And five small faces washed and kissed;
And a broom, and a cloth, and a pot of tea,
    And a laundry list.

All of my life seems a little thing,
    Plus a little thing, with a little name;
Yet most of my life seemed nothing at all
    Before you came . . .

SOME PEOPLE'S CHILDREN

Some will turn cartwheels for cookies,
And some for a soda go wild;
   And many are paid
   With a pink lemonade—
But I have a lollipop child.

Some crave a sled or a scooter,
And some a mechanical toy;
   And lots will succumb
   For a package of gum—
But I have a lollipop boy.

Oh, I've pled and I've plied him with kisses,
With treasure, with theory—but still,
   From the moon to the ground
   Not a thing have I found
That can do what a lollipop will!

VISITOR

When Love came calling yesterday
I was in town, and not about;
He rang a dozen times (they say)—
But I was out.

He carried quite a wondrous stock
(I'm told by neighbors on the block):
Impractical and fragile fare—
A kind of halo for the hair,
An angel's gown with silken ties,
A vial of sparkle for the eyes,
A band of dewdrops for the wrist,
A ring of liquid amethyst.

I would have bought them on the spot,
    Although impractical indeed:
A woman really *needs* a lot
    Of things she doesn't *really* need.

And so when Love comes back to lure
    Me to his trade, my heart to win—
Of this you may be very sure:
    I shall be in.

MENU

How silent does my garden lie
   Without the hum of baby bees;
Now far more fried than even I
   They flank the cocktail anchovies.

The Kangaroo with speed of light
   Has run the race to no avail
And offers in my bowl tonight
   The quickless token of his tail.

In darkling deeps, without alarm,
   Upsetting few, upset by fewer,
The gentle octopod of arm
   Had scarcely thought to grace a skewer.

In Spring the cherry blossoms hung
   That bard and poet did exalt;
To feast the eye, if not the tongue,
   They needed very little salt.

Exotic items widely ranged,
   The avid gourmet must concur;
And yet I wish them all unchanged
   And commonplace as once they were.

HOLD EVERYTHING!

We're gentle folk and kindly folk
    And social-minded too;
And we've never tripped our mothers,
    And we've given dogs their due;
We're very fond of babies—
    We adore the dear papooses
But there comes a time when even saints
    Will dwell on gas and nooses.

We've memorized the formulae
By heart, we'll have you know,
Of every babe from Scranton
To the south of Jericho;
And the albums that we've gazed upon,
If laid out end to end,
Would rim the ring of Saturn
With a ten-mile dividend.

How cute that Susie's sitting up;
How sweet that Tommy's teething!
How gay that Laurelinda laughs;
How nice that Billy's breathing!

We're both berserk with ecstasy . . .
    But, lady, time has flown,
And we've only got two hours left
    To rave about our own!

SUBTLE SUGGESTIONS

FOR MALE SHOPPERS

Some wives have a yen for a toaster
That tosses the toast when it's through;
And some would go wild for a roaster
That might handle a turkey or two . . .
But I'm an impractical maiden
As proven too clearly by this:
    Bizarre as it seems,
    I've been stacking my dreams
On a lipstick, a compact, a kiss.

Expensive's a stove, and a boon it
Would be; and a vacuum or grill
Would be great for the Family Unit,
But where is the personal thrill?
For I am a queer sort of peasant
As any poor husband can see,
Who asks, when you give me a present,
That you give me a present for *me* . . .
So, Love, please recall in your shopping
That I'm an impractical miss
    Who would happily part
    With the whole of my heart
For a lipstick, a compact, a kiss.

PAN

I always said, I always said
   With only wind to hear me:
There'll never be a man can run
   As fast as I, or near me.

There'll never be a man, I said,
   Can pipe the tune to find me;
And if there is, I'll never know—
   He'll be so far behind me.

Today the trees along this road
   Are green with fluted laughter;
The hill is marked by cloven feet—
   And I am running after!

I CANNOT BE ALL THINGS TO YOU

I cannot be all things to you:
    Never the cool of slanted rain;
Never the leafy rise and fall
    Of limbs along a windy lane;

Never the silences of snow,
    The gentle warmth of summer hay;
Never the soothing dark of night,
    Nor subtle light of dawning day.

All that I have is transient fare,
    Brief as the frost in April's wood,
Having no season—like as not
    Here for a moment, gone for good.

Think of me then as what I am,
    Fashioned of earth's reality—
Knowing the gifts I cannot give,
    Knowing the things I cannot be.

I CAN'T GIVE YOU ANYTHING BUT LOVE—
AND SOMETIMES PSYCHOLOGY

Sorry, sweet, if your lambchop's leather;
Sorry, pet, if your coffee's glue;
Sorry, dear, if I accidentally
Dropped my wig in your pot of stew.
Right you are to be miffed and nettled;
Someday I will fuller feed you . . .
(Till that day, will it help a little
To tell you how I muchly need you?)

Grieved am I that your pen is missing;
Crushed I am that your suit's unsent
For thirteen weeks to the corner cleaner;
Sad, oh sad that the fender's bent.
Wrong I was, and the movie's awful;
Someday I will better steer you . . .
(Till that day, will it help a little
To say I melt when I am near you?)

Truly, friend, are your socks all holey?
Really, pal, have the bills run wild?
Honest, chum, did you wed a Woman
And find too late she was still a Child?
But I'll grow up, and I'll grow wiser;
Swear it square on stars above you . . .
(Till that day, will it help a little
To know I deeply, dearly love you?)

VICIOUS CYCLE

I shudder at the icy snow of
Winter; and the less I know of
Hail and sleet, the better. Still, I
Hold my tongue against my will. I
Sense too well when Spring comes round, the
Man I thought was firm will sound the
Hunting horn, and don his wings, and
Soar away to newer things, and
I, with pen chewed to a splinter,
Will write like mad in praise of Winter!

STRAIGHT

Toss the meaning
  To the breeze
And chuck the pat
  Analyses,

And pitch the frown
  From off the brow
Which seeks to grasp
  The What and How.

Take it straight,
  My fond Adonis:
Logic is a curse
  Upon us;

Let's discard
  The mental tricks,
For love and science
  Do not mix;

And why our hearts
  Beat thus and so
I rather would
  We didn't know.

BEHOLD THE YOGI

Behold the Yogi who assails
His problem on a bed of nails
And says with peace upon his eyes:
It feels so good when I arise.

For so it is, my battling beau,
I don't dissolve when off you go,
Nor flip my lid, nor blow my stack:
It feels so good when you come back.

HERE COMES SPRING

Here comes Spring
   in a daisy-sprinkled dirndl
   and open-toe sandals
   and a wide straw hat
   swinging from her arm
   like a basket of flowers.
   What does Spring do
   to look like that?

Where does she go
   when she goes to have her hair done,
   all done up
   with a little green spray?
   It couldn't be Charles,
   and it couldn't be Antoine.
   What's the address,
   and how much does she pay?

Sure, I know:
   it really doesn't matter;
   dreams like that
   are just pure tripe.
   Even if I went,
   they'd say: "Sorry, Madam.
   You haven't got the features,
   and you're not the type."

I'm not Spring
   in a daisy-sprinkled dirndl
   and open-toe sandals
   and a wide straw hat
   swinging from my arm
   like a basket of flowers;
   and that's why they'd *never*
   do my hair like that . . .

TRIOLET OF CONSIDERABLE RELIEF

*"The surest way to catch and keep
a husband is to love him."*
> *—How to Catch a Husband*
> (by G. M. White)

The surest way to catch and keep
   You, darling, is to love you.
What though at housework I'm a creep?
What though my cakes outweigh a jeep?
From you there shouldn't be a peep
   Whilst tendernesses glove you.
The surest way to catch and keep
   You, darling, is to love you.

LINES FOR A TENTH ANNIVERSARY

Plain, the sweatered shoulder
   Without the old corsage;
Unkept, the date for driving—
   The car's in the garage.

Alone, I grace the garden
   'Neath a slim tenth-annual moon,
To the banging of a shutter
   That you'll be fixing—soon.

Past, the days of solitude
   For us to share, my sweet;
The house resounds like City Hall
   With eight demanding feet.

Gone, the time for sentiment;
   Played out, the early game.
Then why do I still quicken
   At the mention of your name?

And why, if life is practical
   And filled with daily fare,
Does my heart do a somersault
   To see you standing there?

I KNOW A MAN

I knew a man who said his love
In rhapsody and roundelay;
A poet, blessed with gifted tongue.
(I wonder where he is today.)

I knew a man, an artisan,
Who took my laughter and my tears
And made of them a silver chain.
(I haven't seen the man for years.)

I know a man — he lives here now,
And I am his forevermore.
He never spoke his love at all;
He planted flowers at my door.

ENEMY

I have no fear of travel:
There's nowhere to travel
From Market Street to Heaven
By wing or by track
That would ever so entice him
That he'd leave his house forever.
He's a lawn-mowing, homey man;
He'd always come back.

I have no fear of women:
Women are equal;
There's just one secret
That all women know.
It has to do with loving—
It's really that simple;
And it's something I found out about
Ages ago.

But when he's sleeping soundly,
That's when I lose him;
Lose him to the darkness
And a world of his own.
Oh, I can handle travel,
And I can handle women—
But I'm beaten by an hour
At midnight, alone.

SHE MAY NOT BE BEAUTIFUL,

BUT SHE SURE IS DUMB

All common sense has slipped me by,
I never sipped at Wisdom's fount;
By two I cannot multiply,
And you should see my bank account;
In any logic-fashioned chain
I represent the missing links;
I cannot even catch a train . . .
He thinks.

I'm quite incapable of thought
(Since it's a function of the mind);
By politics I'm left distraught,
By economics left behind;
No ken have I of business lore,
A dud I am at male affairs;
I do not know that there's a war . . .
He swears.

My head resembles to a T
The well-clichéd and age-old sieve,
And, awed, he asks, "How can it be
She's managed all these years to live?"
Without his reason and his rime,
His guiding hand, I could not cope . . .
That this delusion, sweet, sublime,
He holds until the end of time—
I hope.

WOMEN WITH CHILDREN

Women with children
Have something in common,
Have something in common
That's precious and rare;
And all of their differences,
Whatever differences,
Manage in seconds
To vanish in air.

Women with children
In parks and in drugstores,
At banks, or a food market's
Vegetable stall,
Will stop and will chat
In their own special language
Who otherwise never
Would bother at all.

Women with children
Belong to a union
As vast as an ocean,
As basic as stone;
One day I went shopping
And left mine behind me:
The world had a strange face,
And I was alone.

IV

FOR A CHILD, LEAVING

FOR A CHILD, LEAVING

Go now: I will open
the door for you.
Everything
is in store for you.
There is another room beyond this room;
beyond the circle of my arms and voice,
a further warmth, a further sound.
Rejoice:
the world, my sweet, like any other womb,
is round!

Go now: you are ready to go.
I know —
leavings are lonely.
But look: going is only
a larger kind of living; and I swear:
tomorrow will be better.
(Take your sweater.)

84

Nothing stays:
the ways
of love are always moving;
loving itself is a growing being
as spreading as pain.
Go now, while there is still light for seeing.
(Take your rubbers. It might rain.)

Goodbye now: and remember
what I've said to you:
be nice to the people who ask you in;
they love you, too.
When they give you a gift, smile;
say thank you; even send a card.
(Little things like that make life
        less hard.)

Come on now: nothing is ever really so bad.
Think of what you've had:
it's all there
among your packed belongings:
the rightings and wrongings
of years.
No—please. No tears.
You are Old Enough;
the time to leave is how old Old is.
(Drink lots of orange juice. You know
        how common the cold is.)

Go now: only in part
will I be left behind.
We have shared one heart
and one mind.
No one ever goes alone through any door.
Yes, yes — I shall miss you!
(Wait. Surely there is a minute more.
        I forgot to kiss you.)